Bra

Travel Guide 2023/2024

Max zucks ©

Copyright © 2023

Copyright © by (Max zucks) 2023. All rights reserved. Before this document is duplicated or reproduced in any manner, the publisher's consent must be gained. Therefore, the contents within can neither be stored electronically, transferred, nor kept in a database. Neither in Part nor full can the document be copied, scanned, faxed, or retained without approval from the publisher or creator.

Copyright © 2023

Table of Contents

Table of content
Introduction to Bratislava
History of Bratislava
Geography And Climate
Facts About Bratislava
Reason Why You Should Visit Bratislava
Language
Chapter 1: Planning Your Trip
How To Get To Visit Bratislava
Best Place To Stay In Bratislava
Accommodation options
Transportation options
Best Time To Visit Bratislava
Bratislava Entry and Visa requirements
Chapter 2: Exploring Bratislava
Top Attractions in Bratislava
Outdoor Activities in Bratislava
7 Days Things To Do And See In Bratislava
Shopping And Souvenirs in Bratislava
Popular Shopping Areas in Bratislava
Local Products And Souvenirs

Entertainment And Nightlife Bratislava
Chapter 3: Cultural and Culinary Experiences
Culture And Traditions
Festivals And Event
Food And Drink You May Try in Bratislava
Local Markets And Street Food
Best Restaurant In Bratislava
Useful Phrases And Vocabulary.
Chapter 4: Practical Information
Safety Tips And Precautions
Health Considerations
Local Customs And Etiquette
Currency And Money Matters
How To Save Money In Bratislava Vacation
Things To Pack And Dress Code In Bratislava
Do's And Don'ts In Bratislava
Common Scam In Bratislava
Conclusion

Bratislava is the capital and biggest city of Slovakia, a landlocked nation situated in Focal Europe. Arranged along the banks of the Danube Waterway, Bratislava is the political, financial, and social focus of the country. The city has a long history, more than a thousand years, and it has a unique combination of old-world charm and modern development.

The starting points of Bratislava can be traced back to Roman times, when a sustained settlement called "Bratislava" existed nearby. Over now is the ideal time, the city has been impacted by different societies and has filled in as the capital of various domains, including the Realm of Hungary, the Habsburg government, and Czechoslovakia.

There are currently approximately 450,000 people living in Bratislava. It is a lively city known for its very much safeguarded memorable focus, beautiful palaces, and various compositional styles. The Old Town, also known as "Staré Mesto," is a popular tourist destination due to its colourful buildings, narrow streets, and numerous historic landmarks.

The Bratislava Castle, perched atop a hill with a view of the city, is one of Bratislava's most well-known landmarks. The Slovak National Museum is housed in this magnificent building, which was built in the 9th century and has been used as a military fortress and a royal residence. Another noticeable sight is St. Martin's Church, a dazzling Gothic house of God that assumed a critical part in the nation's set of experiences.

Bratislava offers an extensive variety of social and diversion exercises. The city is home to various historical centres, displays, theatres, and music scenes, exhibiting both conventional and contemporary artistic expressions. Additionally, throughout the year, Bratislava hosts a number of festivals and other events, such as the Christmas Market and the Bratislava Music Festival.

The city's culinary scene is different, affected by Slovak, Hungarian, and Austrian cooking styles. In the numerous cafes and restaurants in the city, visitors can try international cuisine or traditional dishes like bryndzové , which are potato dumplings filled with sheep cheese.

Bratislava has excellent transportation links because it is near the Austrian and Hungarian borders. The Bratislava Airport serves both domestic and international flights, making it easy to get there by plane. Additionally, the city's excellent bus and train connections make it an ideal starting point for exploring the surrounding areas.

In outline, Bratislava is an enthralling city with a rich verifiable legacy, energetic culture, and a developing current personality. Travellers looking for an immersive experience in the centre of Europe will find it to be an appealing destination thanks to its stunning architecture, cultural events, and natural beauty.

History of Bratislava

Over a thousand years ago, various cultures and empires shaped Bratislava's history, which is diverse and complicated. An overview of the city's historical landmarks is as follows:

1. Early Arrivals: The region where Bratislava presently stands has been occupied since antiquated times. During the Roman period, an invigorated settlement called "Bratislava" existed on the site. It was part of the Limes Romanus, a network of fortifications that protected the borders of the Roman Empire, and it was a strategic point along the Danube River.

2. Bygone eras: Bratislava, formerly known as Pressburg or Pozsony, developed into a regional hub for the Great Moravian Empire in the ninth century. In the tenth hundred years, it turned out to be essential for the Realm of Hungary and filled in as the capital from the sixteenth to the nineteenth 100 years. The city

thrived during this period, turning into a significant monetary and political centre point.

3. Habsburg Empire: After the Battle of Mohács in 1526, the Habsburgs took over the Kingdom of Hungary, including Bratislava. As the location of Hungarian kings' and queens' coronations, the city played an important role. Bratislava experienced significant expansion and was adorned with grand palaces, churches, and fortifications under Habsburg rule.

4. Pressburg Period: Between the late 18th century and 1919, Bratislava was referred to as Pressburg in German. During this time, it filled in as the capital of the Pressburg Area inside the Realm of Hungary. Slovaks, Hungarians, Germans, and Jews were among the many ethnic groups that made up the city's diverse population.

5. Czechoslovakia: Bratislava joined the newly formed Czechoslovakia in 1918 after the

Austro-Hungarian Empire was broken up at the end of World War I. It filled in as the capital of Slovakia, which was then a locale inside Czechoslovakia. The city's industrialization progressed during a time of cultural and economic growth.

6. Communist times: Czechoslovakia fell under communist rule following World War II. The city of Bratislava went through critical urbanisation and modern development during this period. Nonetheless, political suppression and monetary difficulties were likewise predominant, affecting the city's turn of events.

7. Slovakia as a nation-state: Czechoslovakia peacefully broke up into two independent nations in 1993: the Czech Republic and Slovakia. Bratislava turned into the capital of the recently framed autonomous Slovakia. The city went through an additional turn of events and modernization, embracing its job

as the political, monetary, and social focus of the country.

Bratislava's growth as a thriving European capital continues today. It has undergone extensive restoration and revitalization projects to embrace modernity while preserving its historical heritage. The city's well-preserved historical centre, architectural landmarks, and cultural traditions all bear witness to its long history, which draws tourists from all over the world.

Geography And Climate

Bratislava is in southwestern Slovakia, close to the Austrian and Hungarian borders. It is in the fertile Danubian Lowland, a region with numerous river systems and flat terrain. The centre of the city is bounded by the Danube River, which runs along its banks.

The Small Carpathian Mountains to the north of Bratislava serve as a picturesque backdrop to the diverse terrain that surrounds the city. These mountains offer open doors for outside exercises like climbing, cycling, and wine sampling in the grape plantations that spot the slants.

Bratislava has a continental climate, with warm summers and winters that range from mild to cold. Here are the overall attributes of the city's environment:

1. Winter months: December through February Bratislava's winters are typically bitterly cold, ranging from below freezing to around 5°C (23°F). Snowfall is normal, however the sum can change from one year to another. January is commonly the coldest month.

2. From March to May, springs: Spring carries milder temperatures to Bratislava, with temperatures slowly climbing from 5°C (41°F) in Spring to around 15°C (59°F) in May. The weather conditions can be variable during this season, with incidental downpour showers.

3. From June to August, summers: Summers in Bratislava are warm to sweltering, with temperatures going from 20°C (68°F) to 30°C (86°F). July and August are the most sizzling months, and intermittent heat waves can push temperatures above 30°C (86°F). Summer typically experiences the most precipitation, with regular downpours.

4. Falls (September to November): In Bratislava, autumn temperatures gradually fall. September is still generally warm, with temperatures around 20°C (68°F), while November brings temperatures going from 0°C (32°F) to 10°C (50°F). The season is marked by vivid foliage and occasional precipitation.

Throughout the year, Bratislava experiences moderate precipitation, with the wettest months being June, July, and August. The city gets about 2,000 hours of sunshine every year, and there are more hours of daylight in the summer.

Overall, Bratislava is a pleasant place to visit because of its location and climate. There are distinct seasonal changes and a variety of urban and natural landscapes to explore.

Facts About Bratislava

Certainly! Some interesting facts about Bratislava are as follows:

1. Capital City: Slovakia's largest and capital city is Bratislava. Additionally, it serves as the nation's cultural, economic, and administrative hub.

2. Area and Boundaries: Bratislava is in southwestern Slovakia, close to the Austrian and Hungarian borders. The Austrian capital, Vienna, is somewhere around 60 kilometres (37 miles) west of Bratislava, making it one of the nearest capital city matches on the planet.

3. Danube Stream: The city is situated along the banks of the Danube Waterway, one of Europe's significant streams. The Danube assumes a fundamental part in the city's set of experiences, transportation, and diversion.

4. Multicultural Personality: Bratislava's multicultural past is shaped by a variety of ethnic groups. The city has generally been home to Slovaks, Hungarians, Germans, and Jews, among others. Architecture, customs, and cuisine all reflect this diverse cultural background.

5. Royal celebration Site: For nearly three centuries, Hungarian kings and queens were crowned in Bratislava. The crowning liturgy

services occurred in the St. Martin's Basilica, and the Royal gems were kept in the city's palace.

6. Castle of Bratislava: A prominent landmark is the recognizable Bratislava Castle, which is perched on a hill overlooking the city. The castle was built in the 9th century and has been used as a military fortress and a royal residence throughout its history. Today, it houses the Slovak Public Gallery.

7. Deck for Observing UFOs: The SNP Extension, otherwise called the New Scaffold, includes a remarkable UFO-formed structure at its top. The city and the surrounding area can be seen from this UFO Observation Deck.

8. Place of the film: Several international films, including "The Peacemaker," starring George Clooney and Nicole Kidman, and Eli Roth's "Hostel," were filmed in Bratislava.

9. Devin Palace: Found a couple of kilometres from the downtown area, Devin Palace is a very much saved middle age post arranged at the juncture of the Danube and Morava waterways. It offers stunning views of the surrounding landscapes and is a popular tourist spot.

10. Cycling-Accommodating City: Bratislava has fostered a broad organisation of cycling ways, making it a city that welcomes bikes. The city's level territory and lovely riverside courses make cycling a well known movement for the two local people and guests.

Bratislava is an intriguing destination to explore because these facts provide just a glimpse into its vibrant history, cultural diversity, and distinctive characteristics.

Reason Why You Should Visit Bratislava Language

Bratislava, Slovakia's capital, is well worth a visit for a number of compelling reasons. Certainly one of them is language. This is why:

1. Language Training: When you go to Bratislava, you can learn the Slovak language all by yourself. Although English is widely spoken in tourist areas and among younger generations, Slovak is still spoken in everyday life. Slovak is the official language of Slovakia. Engaging in conversation in the local language can help you learn about the culture, connect with the locals, and enhance your trip.

2. Cultural Discovery: Language is an important part of a country's culture, and if you go to Bratislava, you can get a firsthand look at Slovak culture. You can see the distinctive language expressions, idioms, and customs of the locals as you explore the city. From road signs to discussions at bistros,

you'll experience Slovak language components that add to the social embroidered artwork of the city.

3. Legitimate Collaborations: Realising a couple of fundamental Slovak expressions can go far in laying out associations with local people. While many individuals in Bratislava communicate in English, endeavouring to communicate in Slovak shows your advantage in their way of life and can open ways to credible connections. Locals will appreciate your efforts to speak their language, whether you're asking for directions or ordering food at a traditional restaurant.

4. Cultural Assets: Bratislava is a great starting point for exploring Slovakia's extensive cultural heritage. Numerous comprehensive developments, celebrations, and exhibitions in the city praise the Slovak language, writing, and expressions. You can witness the beauty and significance of the Slovak language in preserving and promoting

the nation's cultural identity by attending these events.

5. Etymological Variety: Bratislava's remarkable geological area close to the boundaries of Austria and Hungary permits you to encounter phonetic variety. Due to the region's multiculturalism and historical influences, you might also hear German and Hungarian in addition to Slovak. This etymological blend establishes a dynamic and improving climate for language fans and explorers.

Overall, your time in Bratislava will be richer and deeper because of the language factor. It facilitates authentic interactions, cultural exploration, and a deeper comprehension of Slovakia's heritage. Therefore, take advantage of the unique opportunity to visit a city where language plays a significant role and embrace the linguistic adventure.

Chapter 1: Planning Your Trip

Part 1: Planning a Trip to Bratislava Can Be Exciting Planning a trip to Bratislava can be exciting. Whether you're a set of experiences buff, an admirer of engineering, or essentially looking for another European objective, Bratislava offers a novel mix of old-world appeal and current charm. This chapter will walk you through the essential steps you need to take when planning your trip to Bratislava to make it easy and enjoyable.

1. Decide the Best Opportunity to Visit: Consider the season you intend to visit Bratislava. There are various seasons in the city, each with its own attractions. Milder weather, fewer people, and vibrant foliage are all part of spring (March to May) and autumn (September to November). Summer, which lasts from June to August, is the busiest time for tourists, with warm temperatures and the possibility of more rain. Winter (December to

February) is colder, however it offers the valuable chance to encounter the city's merry climate and Christmas markets.

2. Length of Stay:
Set a time limit for your stay in Bratislava. Depending on your interests and available time, a typical visit can last anywhere from a few days to a week. Keep in mind that Bratislava's small size allows you to see the main attractions in a shorter time, but if you want to see more of the city and the surrounding area, you might want to stay for longer.

3. Travel Archives and Section Prerequisites:
Guarantee that your movement archives are all together. Depending on your nationality, determine whether you require a visa to enter Slovakia. Check to see that your passport still has validity for at least six months after the date you plan to leave. To avoid any last-minute problems, research the most

recent entry requirements and visa regulations for Slovakia.

4. Transportation:
Find out the best route to Bratislava. Air, road, and rail connections serve the city well. If you are arriving by plane, look for flights to Bratislava Airport or Vienna International Airport, which is close by and convenient. If you prefer to travel by bus or train, look into how to get to Bratislava from nearby cities or countries.

5. Accommodation:
Think about your convenience inclinations and spending plan. There are many choices in Bratislava, from expensive hotels to cheap hostels and apartments. The downtown area, especially the Old Town (Staré Mesto), is a well known region to remain because of its closeness to significant attractions.
Examination and book your convenience ahead of time to get your favoured decision.

6. Attractions and sights to see:
Make a list of Bratislava's must-see sights. Incorporate tourist spots like Bratislava Palace, St. Martin's Basilica, Michael's Entryway, and the UFO Perception Deck. Investigate the beguiling roads of the Old Town, visit historical centres and displays, and consider taking a boat visit along the Danube Waterway. Plan your agenda in view of your inclinations, permitting time for both famous sights and off in an unexpected direction.

7. Cuisine and Culture of the Area:
Research the neighbourhood culture, customs, and decorum of Bratislava. To show respect to the locals, familiarise yourself with Slovak customs, greetings, and dining etiquette. Try bryndzové , which is potato dumplings with sheep cheese, , which is cabbage soup, and , which is a sweet pastry. Slovak food can be enjoyed at a variety of local eateries, cafes, and markets.

8. Currency and budgeting:

Make a trip budget that includes things like lodging, transportation, meals, sightseeing, and any additional costs. The Euro (EUR) is Slovakia's official currency. Research the ebb and flow trade rates and consider conveying some neighbourhood money for little buys. Most places accept credit cards, but it's a good idea to have some cash on hand for places that might not.

9. Health and Safety:
Likewise with any excursion, focus on your security and prosperity. Learn about the hospitals and emergency numbers in your area. Check in the event that you want any immunizations prior to venturing out to Slovakia and think about buying head out protection to cover any unexpected conditions.

10. Learn the Essential Slovene Phrases:
Even though most people in Bratislava speak English, knowing a few basic Slovak phrases can be helpful and show that you appreciate

24

the local language. Practise good tidings, please and thank you, and straightforward expressions for requesting food or requesting headings.

You will be well-prepared to embark on a memorable journey to this captivating city if you follow these steps and plan your trip to Bratislava in advance. Part 2 will dive into the features and must-see attractions of Bratislava, assisting you with making an astonishing agenda for your visit.

How To Get To Visit Bratislava

There are a variety of ways to get to Bratislava, depending on where you are and what you like to do. Here are the most well-known ways of getting to Bratislava:

1. By Air:

The primary airport serving the city is Bratislava Airport (Letisko M. R. tefánika). It is a convenient alternative for travellers because it offers flights both domestically and internationally. From the air terminal, you can take a taxi, public transport, or pre-booked air terminal exchange to arrive at the downtown area, which is roughly 9 kilometres (5.6 miles) away.

On the other hand, Vienna Global Air terminal in Austria is situated around 60 kilometres (37 miles) west of Bratislava. Numerous worldwide voyagers decide to travel to Vienna and afterward take an immediate transport, train, or taxi to Bratislava, which requires about 60 minutes.

2. On Trains:
By train, Bratislava is well connected to a number of European cities. Assuming you're going from adjacent nations like Austria, Hungary, Czech Republic, or Poland, there are immediate train associations with

Bratislava. "Bratislava hlavná stanica," or "Bratislava Main Station," is the name of Bratislava's primary train station. By taxi or public transportation, you can easily reach the city centre from there.

3. By Bus:
Global and homegrown transports likewise serve Bratislava, offering reasonable and advantageous transportation choices. Eurolines and FlixBus are two significant transport administrators with courses interfacing Bratislava to various European urban communities. The "Bratislava Autobusová stanica" (Bratislava Bus Station) is the main bus station in Bratislava. It is close to the city centre.

4. By Car:
Assuming that you lean toward the adaptability of driving, you can arrive at Bratislava via vehicle. The city is very much associated with adjoining nations by means of expressways. The D1 motorway joins

Bratislava with Vienna, while the D2 motorway connects it to Budapest. Before setting out on your journey, it is essential to verify the specific driving laws, tolls, and parking options.

5. Take a River Cruise:
For a special and beautiful methodology, consider showing up in Bratislava by means of a waterway journey along the Danube Stream. Numerous stream voyage organisations offer schedules that incorporate Bratislava as a stop en route. You can walk around the city or take the bus once you dock at the Bratislava Passenger Port.

When you show up in Bratislava, the city has a proficient and very much associated public vehicle framework containing transports, cable cars, and trolleybuses, making it simple to explore and investigate the different attractions.

Pick the transportation mode that best suits your inclinations, spending plan, and area, and partake in your excursion to the dazzling city of Bratislava.

Best Place To Stay In Bratislava

With regards to picking the best spot to remain in Bratislava, it generally relies upon your inclinations and interests. The following are some well-known locations that provide diverse experiences:

1. Old Town (Staré Mesto):
The Old Town is the notable heart of Bratislava and a famous decision for some guests. It is described by restricted cobblestone roads, brilliant structures, and an enchanting air. Remaining in this space permits you to be within a walking distance of significant attractions like Bratislava Palace, St. Martin's Church building, Michael's Entryway, and the Primary Square. There are

numerous choices for lodging, including apartments, guesthouses, and boutique hotels.

2. Palace Slope (Hradná hora):
Castle Hill has stunning views of Bratislava and the Danube River and is just above the Old Town. If you stay in this area, you'll be close to Bratislava Castle and its gardens. While it is somewhat calmer than the Old Town, it offers a quiet and beautiful environment. This area is home to a number of hotels and guesthouses, making it easy to unwind after a long day of exploration.

3. Eurovea and Riverfront:
Along the Danube River, Eurovea is a contemporary waterfront development with a mix of residential, commercial, and entertainment spaces. Stylish hotels with river views can be found in this area, which is well connected to the city centre by foot or public transportation. You can easily get to the Eurovea Shopping Center, riverside

promenades, and a lot of restaurants and cafes if you stay here.

4. Petržalka:

The residential area known as Petralka can be found on the opposite bank of the Danube River from the city centre. With a variety of reasonably priced lodging options, including hotels and apartments, it provides a more residential and localised experience. While it isn't in the prompt downtown area, it is very much associated with open vehicles, permitting you to arrive at the attractions inside a short excursion.

Consider factors like nearness to attractions, financial plan, favoured air, and comfort while picking the best spot to remain in Bratislava. The city's small size makes it easy to see and enjoy its many attractions and experiences, regardless of where you choose to live.

Accommodation opinion

Although I am merely an AI language model, I am able to provide you with some general information regarding Bratislava's lodging options.

Bratislava offers a scope of convenience choices to suit various inclinations and spending plans. The following are a couple of kinds of convenience you can consider:

1. Hotels: Bratislava has various inns, going from financial plan well disposed choices to extravagance foundations. On-site restaurants, fitness centres, and concierge services are frequently offered by hotels. They can be tracked down in different regions of the city, including the Old Town, Palace Slope, Eurovea, and different areas.

2. Bed and breakfasts and guesthouses: Guesthouses and B&Bs offer a more close and genial climate. They are typically run by local hosts who provide individualised service

and tend to be smaller in scale. These accommodations are available in various parts of the city, including the Old Town and the neighbourhoods that surround it.

3. Vacation Rentals and Apartments: On the off chance that you lean toward a more free and self-cooking choice, you can think about leasing a condo or excursion rental. These facilities give you more space, a kitchenette or full kitchen, and the adaptability to make your own timetable. They are accessible all through the city, remembering the Old Town, Palace Slope, and other neighbourhoods.

4. Hostels: There are a few hostels in Bratislava that cater to travellers on a budget and those seeking a social setting. Lodgings frequently offer dorm style rooms as well as confidential rooms, collective regions, and shared kitchen offices. They are typically found in the Old Town and other nearby areas of the city's centre.

While picking convenience, consider factors like area, closeness to attractions, financial plan, conveniences, and the sort of involvement you like. To learn more about a specific lodging, its facilities, and the experiences of previous guests, it is recommended to read reviews and use booking platforms.

Eventually, the best convenience choice for you will rely upon your own inclinations, travel style, and financial plan.

Transportation options

There are a number of transportation options in Bratislava for getting around the city and seeing the surrounding area. Here are the fundamental methods of transportation you can consider:

1. Public Vehicle:

Buses, trams, and trolleybuses make up Bratislava's extensive and efficient public transportation system. These modes of transportation cover the entire city and make it easy to get to different neighbourhoods and places of interest. You can buy tickets at ticket machines, public vehicle booths, or through versatile applications. Upon boarding, either validate your ticket or follow the provided ticketing instructions.

2. Walking:
Bratislava's smaller size and walker amicable format make it an optimal city to investigate by walking. It is simple to walk to many of the main attractions, including the Old Town. Walking around the limited roads permits you to submerge yourself in the city's appeal, find unlikely treasures, and take in the compositional magnificence.

3. Cycling:
Bratislava has created a network of bike paths and bike lanes because cycling is a popular

mode of transportation. You can lease bikes from different rental shops and use them to investigate the city's milestones or adventure further into the encompassing open country. Remember that cycling guidelines and traffic rules ought to be observed for your security.

4. Taxis:
In Bratislava, there are a lot of taxis that can be rented on the street or booked through taxi services or ride-hailing apps. To ensure fair pricing and dependable service, it is recommended to use reputable taxi services or dependable apps. Make sure the metre is used during the ride and always look for the taxi's official identification.

5. Rental Car:
Renting a car in Bratislava is an option if you value independence and flexibility. There are a number of car rental businesses with locations in the city and at the airport. It is essential to familiarise yourself with the Bratislava traffic laws, parking options, and

any particular driving requirements or restrictions.

6. Tours for Sightseeing:
Bratislava offers different directed touring visits, including strolling visits, transport visits, boat visits along the Danube Waterway, and even Segway visits. These tours allow you to explore the city's highlights with the convenience of a knowledgeable guide and provide insightful commentary.

When choosing the best mode of transportation in Bratislava, take into account your specific requirements, preferences, and travel distance. A good way to get around the city and make the most of your time there is to use a variety of different modes of transportation.

Best Time To Visit Bratislava

Your personal preferences and the kind of experience you're looking for will largely determine when is the best time to visit Bratislava. Each season in Bratislava has its own appeal and remarkable contributions. Here is a breakdown of the various seasons to assist you with choosing:

1. March through May:
Spring in Bratislava brings gentle temperatures, blooming blossoms, and a reviving air. After the winter, the city starts to come to life, and you can take nice walks through the parks and gardens. In addition, there are fewer tourists in spring than in summer, making it easier to visit attractions. Nonetheless, remember that incidental precipitation is normal during this season.

2. From June to August, summer:
Because of the warm, sunny weather, summer is Bratislava's busiest tourist season. The typical temperatures range from 20°C to

30°C (68°F to 86°F). This is an extraordinary opportunity to appreciate outside exercises, visit outdoors occasions, and loosen up in the city's parks and riverside promenades. The mid year months additionally bring energetic road celebrations and lively nightlife. Nonetheless, it's essential to take note that well known vacationer locales can be packed during this time, and costs for facilities and flights might be higher.

3. September through November:
The pleasant temperatures of autumn in Bratislava range from mild to cool. An idyllic atmosphere is created by the city's beautiful fall foliage. Autumn is a wonderful time to visit the city's parks and gardens, take in cultural events, and eat seasonal fare. The traveller swarms start to disseminate during this season, offering a more peaceful encounter. Pack appropriately because November can be cooler and wetter.

4. Winter: November through February

Bratislava's winter temperatures range from 24°F to 43°F, with an average range of -4°C to 6°C. Christmas markets, ice skating rinks, and holiday decorations give the city a cosy and festive vibe during the holidays. You can enjoy the city's cultural traditions and hearty Slovak cuisine when you visit in the winter. However, keep in mind that some attractions and outdoor activities may be closed during this time, so bring warm clothing.

In outline, the best opportunity to visit Bratislava relies upon your inclinations for climate, swarm levels, and explicit exercises or occasions you wish to encounter. Summer is ideal for outdoor activities and lively events, while spring and autumn offer milder temperatures and fewer tourists. Winter is ideally suited for embracing the city's bubbly climate. Think about your needs and pick the season that lines up with your ideal travel insight.

Bratislava Entry and Visa requirements

Passage and visa prerequisites for Bratislava, Slovakia, may fluctuate relying upon your identity and the reason and span of your visit. The following is some general information regarding Bratislava's entry requirements and visa requirements:

1. Unrestricted Entry:
Residents of numerous nations, including the European Association (EU) part expresses, the US, Canada, Australia, New Zealand, and a few others, don't need a visa to enter Slovakia for the travel industry or transient visits. In most cases, visitors from these nations do not need a visa to visit Slovakia for up to 90 days within a 180-day period. However, as visa exemptions may vary, it is essential to verify your nationality's specific requirements.

2. Schengen Region:
The Schengen Area is a group of 26 European nations with no more internal border controls. Slovakia is one of these countries. In the event that you hold a legitimate Schengen visa, you can enter Slovakia and travel inside the whole Schengen Region without requiring an extra visa. The Schengen visa considers a stay of as long as 90 days inside a 180-day time span.

3. Validity of a passport:
Check to see that the expiration date on your passport is at least six months after your planned departure date from Slovakia. Check the validity of your passport in advance and renew it if necessary.

4. Visa Application:
On the off chance that you are a citizen of a country that requires a visa to enter Slovakia, you should apply for a Schengen visa at the international safe haven or department of

Slovakia in your nation of origin or the nation where you lawfully live. A completed visa application form, a current passport, proof of travel insurance, proof of accommodation, and proof of financial means are typically required for the application process. The most recent and specific visa requirements can be found on the official website of the Slovak embassy or consulate in your country.

5. Permits for Residence:
A residence permit may be required if you intend to stay in Slovakia for an extended period of time for work, school, or family reasons. Home licences are given by the Unfamiliar Police in Slovakia, and the application cycle shifts relying upon the motivation behind your visit. For more information about the requirements and procedures for obtaining a residence permit, it is suggested that you speak with either the Foreign Police in Slovakia or the Slovak Embassy or Consulate in your home country.

For up-to-date information on entry and visa requirements specific to your nationality and travel circumstances, it is essential to check the official government websites or consult the relevant Slovak authorities, such as the embassy or consulate.

Chapter 2: Exploring Bratislava

Section 2: Investigating Bratislava

Bratislava, the capital city of Slovakia, is loaded up with verifiable milestones, social fortunes, and dynamic areas ready to be investigated. In this section, we will dive into the features and must-see attractions of Bratislava, assisting you with making an astonishing schedule for your visit.

1. Castle of Bratislava:
Roosted on a slope sitting above the city, Bratislava Palace is a notable image of the

city. Bratislava and the Danube River can be seen from the castle's four corner towers and distinctive white walls. Investigate the palace's inside, visit the Slovak Public Historical centre housed inside its walls, and drench yourself in the city's set of experiences.

2. Cathedral of St. Martin:
St. Martin's Cathedral is a magnificent Gothic cathedral in the centre of the Old Town that played a significant role in Slovakia's history. Respect its amazing tower and step inside to wonder about the dazzling inside, including the Sanctuary of St. John the Almoner and the crowning liturgy house of prayer. Take advantage of the opportunity to scale the cathedral's tower for unobstructed city views.

3. The Gate and Tower of Michael:
As the main safeguarded middle age door in Bratislava, Michael's Entryway is a memorable milestone worth visiting. The charming Michalská Street can be accessed through the gate, which was built in the 14th

century. Take in panoramic views of the Old Town and beyond by scaling the tower.

4. Primate's Castle:
Take a tour of the primate's palace, an elegant neoclassical structure that houses the mayor of Bratislava. Investigate the shocking Lobby of Mirrors and the wonderful nurseries. The famous Primatial Hall, which is decorated with exquisite English tapestries of scenes from Don Quixote, is also located in the palace.

5. Slovak Public Theater:
The Slovak National Theatre is a must-see for anyone who enjoys the arts. Opera, ballet, and drama performances take place in this magnificent building. Immerse yourself in the vibrant atmosphere of the theatre and enjoy the world-class productions that showcase Slovakia's cultural diversity.

6. Devin Palace:
Devin Castle is a striking mediaeval fortress at the confluence of the Danube and Morava

rivers, just a short distance from Bratislava. Take in the breathtaking views, explore the castle's ruins, and learn about its lengthy history. You can arrive at Devin Palace by boat, transport, or bicycle, making it an ideal road trip from Bratislava.

7. Old Town (Staré Mesto):
Take in the atmosphere of Bratislava's historic centre as you meander through its cobbled streets. Appreciate the pastel-shaded structures, visit beguiling bistros and eateries, and peruse store shops. Relax in one of the charming squares, visit the Maximilian Fountain, and discover secret courtyards.

8. St. Elizabeth's Church Blue Church:
The Blue Church is a one-of-a-kind masterpiece of Art Nouveau that stands out for its sky-blue exterior. Step inside this compositional work of art to wonder about its unpredictable adornments and pastel-blue variety conspire. A truly undiscovered

treasure, The Blue Church provides a tranquil and captivating experience.

9. Promenade along the Danube:
Enjoy the picturesque views of the Danube River and its bridges as you take a leisurely stroll along the promenade. This beautiful region offers parks, open air bistros, and the opportunity to notice the notorious UFO Perception Deck roosted on the SNP Extension.

10. Slovak Public Display:
For workmanship lovers, a visit to the Slovak Public Display is strongly suggested. The gallery has a large collection of artwork from Slovakia and around the world, from various periods and styles. Investigate the super durable and transitory shows to acquire bits of knowledge into the dynamic Slovak workmanship scene.

This part has featured a portion of the top attractions and encounters in Bratislava.

Nonetheless, the city offers much more to find, including dynamic business sectors, present day locale, and a vivacious culinary scene. Make your itinerary specific to your interests, take in the city's rich history and culture, and take in Bratislava's distinctive charm.

Top Attractions in Bratislava

The captivating attractions in Bratislava, Slovakia's capital, highlight the city's vibrant culture, stunning architecture, and long history. Bratislava's top attractions include the following:

1. Castle of Bratislava: Bratislava Castle is a well-known landmark that sits atop a hill with a view of the city. Investigate the palace's authentic shows, respect its excellent design,

and appreciate all encompassing perspectives on the city.

2. Cathedral of St. Martin: The towering spire of this magnificent Gothic cathedral in the city centre is well-known. Step inside to respect its inside and visit the grave where a few Hungarian lords were crowned.

3. Old Town (Staré Mesto): The memorable Old Town is an enchanting region loaded up with cobblestone roads, beautiful structures, and middle age design. Visit historic squares like Main Square and Hviezdoslavovo Square, wander its narrow alleys, and take in the lively atmosphere.

4. Gate of Michael: Michael's Gate is a significant landmark in Bratislava because it is the only intact mediaeval gate there. Move to the highest point of the pinnacle for all encompassing perspectives on the city.

5. The Primal Palace: This neoclassical royal residence houses the City chairman's Office and elements of the dazzling Corridor of Mirrors. Take a look inside and around the palace's gardens.

6. St. Elizabeth's Church Blue Church: The Blue Church is a one-of-a-kind masterpiece of Art Nouveau, distinguished by the sky-blue exterior and decorative elements. Step inside to wonder about its delightfully created inside.

7. Deck for Observing UFOs: Situated on the SNP Extension, the UFO Perception Deck offers amazing all encompassing perspectives on Bratislava. Partake in a feast or a beverage at the housetop eatery while taking in the shocking vistas.

8. Devin Palace: Devin Castle is an impressive fortress at the confluence of the Danube and Morava rivers, a short distance from Bratislava. Investigate its remains,

appreciate grand perspectives, and find out about its rich history.

9. National Theatre of Slovakia: This delightful auditorium has show, expressive dance, and show exhibitions. Through its world-class productions, discover Slovakia's cultural diversity.

10. National Gallery of Slovakia: Investigate the Slovak Public Exhibition to see a broad assortment of Slovak and global workmanship. Find works crossing different periods and styles.

These are just a few of the many things to do in Bratislava. Because the city is so small, it's easy to walk around these places and find hidden gems. Discover the best places to visit in Bratislava and immerse yourself in the city's distinctive mix of history, culture, and stunning architecture.

Outdoor Activities in Bratislava

The capital of Slovakia, Bratislava, has a lot to offer outdoor enthusiasts who love nature, adventure, and want to see the beautiful countryside that surrounds the city. In and around Bratislava, enjoy the following outdoor pursuits:

1. Cycling: Bratislava brags a broad organisation of cycling ways, making it an optimal city for trekking. Explore the city's parks, riverside promenades, and cycling trails on a bicycle. The Little Carpathian Mountains north of Bratislava likewise offer tourist detours for additional accomplished cyclists.

2. Hiking: Hiking in the Small Carpathian Mountains near Bratislava is a great activity. Take a hike through lush forests, picturesque vineyards, and charming villages by lacing up your hiking boots. Some famous climbing

objections incorporate Devín Palace, Kamzík Slope, and Červený Kameň Palace.

3. Cruises on the Danube River: Experience the magnificence of the Danube Stream by taking a waterway journey. Browse touring travels that give staggering perspectives on Bratislava's horizon and milestones or leave on a more extended voyage to investigate the Danube's picturesque stretches and visit close by towns and urban communities.

4. Canoeing and kayaking: Investigate the streams around Bratislava by kayaking or paddling on the Danube Waterway or its feeders. Paddle along the waterway, partake in the tranquil environmental elements, and take in the beautiful scenes. There are a number of tour companies that offer guided canoe and kayak trips.

5. SUP: Stand-Up Paddleboarding Take a look at stand-up paddleboarding on the calm Danube River. Exploring the river and taking

in the city from a new angle with a SUP is a relaxing and enjoyable activity. Rentals and directed visits are accessible.

6. Forest Park of Bratislava: Bratislava Forest Park, also known as Bratislavsky park, is a green haven just outside of the city that can be found at the foothills of the Small Carpathians. Appreciate strolling or running on the backwoods trails, have an outing, or essentially unwind in the midst of nature.

7. Golf: Golfers can start their round at one of the nearby courses. Courses, for example, Dark Waterway Golf Resort and Golf and Nation Club Bernolák offer wonderful settings and difficulties for players of all expertise levels.

8. Horseback Riding: On horseback, take in the surrounding countryside of Bratislava. A few equestrian habitats and farms offer pony riding encounters for all levels, permitting you

to partake in the grand scenes in a one of a kind way.

9. Greenhouses: Visit the Greenhouses of Comenius College or the Bratislava ZOO, the two of which offer tranquil open air spaces to see the value in assorted verdure.

10. Picnicking and Outside Unwinding: Exploit the city's parks and green spaces for picnics, sunbathing, or partaking in a comfortable walk. Sad Janka Kráa, Elezná Studnika, and Medická Záhrada are among the most well-liked parks.

While you're in Bratislava, these outdoor activities give you a chance to connect with nature, take in stunning scenery, and have fun. Whether you favour an adrenaline-sipping experience or a quiet retreat, there's something for everybody to appreciate in the nature of Bratislava.

7 Days Things To Do And See In Bratislava

If you only have seven days to spend in Bratislava, you'll have plenty of time to see the city's highlights, immerse yourself in its culture, and explore the surrounding areas. A suggested itinerary for a week in Bratislava is as follows:

Day 1: Start your trip off with a visit to the charming Old Town (Staré Mesto). Visit milestones like St. Martin's Church building, Michael's Entryway, and the Primary Square. Take in the atmosphere of this historic district as you meander through the cobblestone streets, take in the vibrant architecture, and admire it all.
- Partake in a feast at a customary Slovak eatery and attempt nearby strengths like bryndzové halušky (potato dumplings with sheep cheddar) or (cabbage soup).

Day 2: Bratislava Palace and Danube Waterway
- Start your day by visiting Bratislava Palace. From the castle grounds, you can take in panoramic views, learn about the city's history, and explore its exhibits.
- Go for a comfortable stroll along the Danube Stream promenade, stopping to respect the notable UFO Perception Deck and partaking in the grand perspectives.
Take a Danube river cruise to see the city's skyline and take in the peace and quiet of the river.

Day 3: Devin Castle and Wine Tasting: Devin Castle is just a short drive from Bratislava. Take a day trip there. Take in the stunning views of the Danube and Morava rivers as you explore the castle's ruins and learn about its history.
- Pay a visit to a local winery near Bratislava in the Small Carpathian wine region. Take a visit through the grape plantations, find out

about Slovak wines, and enjoy wine sampling meetings.

Day 4: Social Features
- Go through the day investigating the city's social features. For a deeper comprehension of Slovak culture and history, pay a visit to the Museum of City History, the Slovak National Theatre, or the Slovak National Gallery.
- Take a walking tour with a local guide to learn more about the city's history, architecture, and landmarks.

Day 5: Open air Experience
- Participate in open air exercises close to Bratislava. In the Small Carpathian Mountains, you can go biking or hiking. Visit charming villages, explore picturesque trails, and take in the stunning natural surroundings. For a unique water-based adventure, think about kayaking, canoeing, or stand-up paddleboarding on the Danube River.

Day 6: Explore the contemporary side of Bratislava with Modern Bratislava and Eurovea. Shop, eat, and unwind along the Danube River at Eurovea, a bustling waterfront community.
- Explore cutting-edge structures like the Slovak Radio Building and the SNP Bridge with its UFO Observation Deck.
- For a taste of Art Nouveau, check out contemporary art galleries or the unique Blue Church.

Day 7: Neighbourhood Encounters and Goodbye
- Go through your last day encountering neighbourhood life. Taste and purchase local produce, traditional foods, and crafts at local markets like the Old Market Hall.
- To unwind and appreciate nature, take a leisurely stroll through one of Bratislava's parks, such as Sad Janka Kráa or Elezná Studnicka.
- Celebrate the end of your trip with a last Slovak meal and a toast to Bratislava.

This schedule gives a blend of verifiable, social, outside, and current encounters, permitting you to find the best of Bratislava soon. Depending on your interests and preferences, you are free to modify the activities and investigate additional attractions.

Shopping And Souvenirs in Bratislava

There are a lot of options for souvenirs and shopping in Bratislava, from traditional Slovak goods to international brands. Consider the following popular shopping areas and common souvenirs:

1. Staré Mastro's Old Town:
The Old Town of Bratislava is a great shopping destination, offering a blend of shop stores, keepsake shops, and nearby

craftsmans. You can find conventional Slovak specialties, craftsmanship, and extraordinary keepsakes in this beguiling region.

2. Venturska Street and Obchodná Street:
These roads in the downtown area are fixed with shops selling dresses, embellishments, and other style things. Local designers as well as international brands exhibit their creations.

3. Aupark and Eurovea:
Modern shopping centres like Eurovea and Aupark have a wide range of shops, from electronics and home decor to fashion and beauty. These shopping centres are suitable for a comprehensive shopping experience because they offer a mix of domestic and international brands.

4. Kamenné Square Market:
Kamenné Square Market, which is close to the Old Town, is a great place to find traditional Slovak food items like honey, jams, cheeses, sausages, and local wines. You can

also look at stalls that sell ceramics, handicrafts, and souvenirs.

5. Folk Art from Slovakia:
Keep an eye out for handmade ceramics, wooden toys, embroidered textiles, pottery, and other traditional Slovak folk crafts. These unique and authentic souvenirs frequently reflect the country's rich cultural heritage.

6. Conventional Food and Beverages:
Think about reintroducing some traditional Slovak foodstuffs, like sheep cheese, pálenka, or fruit brandy, honey, and Slovak wines. These neighbourhood delights can be found in specialty food shops or markets.

7. People Ensembles and Apparel:
Look for shops that sell folk costumes, accessories, and embroidered clothing if you're interested in traditional Slovak clothing. These pieces feature the farm raised people's practices and make for unmistakable keepsakes.

8. Slovak Literature and Music:
Visit bookstores to peruse a selection of Slovak books, including translations and works by Slovak authors, if you are interested in Slovak music or literature. You can likewise search for Compact discs highlighting conventional Slovak music or contemporary specialists.

When purchasing souvenirs, remember to check for authenticity and quality. Search for names or signs demonstrating that the items are handcrafted or privately created. Furthermore, the Old Market Corridor in the Old Town and the bigger retail outlets referenced before frequently have committed segments for conventional Slovak items and gifts.

When you go shopping in Bratislava, you can learn about local craftsmanship, traditional goods, and one-of-a-kind keepsakes that capture the essence of Slovakia's culture and heritage.

Popular Shopping Areas in Bratislava

There are numerous shopping areas in Bratislava where you can find a mix of local goods, international brands, and one-of-a-kind finds. Bratislava's most well-known shopping districts are as follows:

1. St. Obchodná:
Situated in the downtown area, Obchodná Road is a clamouring shopping road known for its scope of shops and stores. Here, you'll find a blend of worldwide design brands, shoe stores, bookshops, and niche stores. It's a lively neighbourhood with cafes and restaurants, making it ideal for shopping.

2. Eurovea:

Along the Danube River, there is a contemporary shopping mall called Eurovea. It has a wide range of shops, including ones selling home decor, electronics, and fashion. You can likewise track down a determination of eateries, bistros, and diversion choices in this shopping complex.

3. Aupark:
Another well-known shopping centre near the city centre is Aupark. It has numerous shops that sell clothes, accessories, electronics, and household goods. Aupark likewise has a film, diversion offices, and a food court, giving a total shopping experience.

4. Market in Kamenné Square:
Kamenné Square Market is a conventional market close to the Old Town, where you can track down new produce, neighbourhood items, crafted works, and trinkets. You can get a taste of traditional Slovak cuisine and learn about the local culture there.

5. Bratislava's Old Town:
The Old Town of Bratislava is not only full of history and beautiful architecture, but it also has many shops and boutiques. You'll find a blend of gift shops, distinctive specialties, style stores, gems stores, and that's only the tip of the iceberg. Unique finds can be found in the tucked-away courtyards and tucked-away streets.

6. Malls:
Notwithstanding Eurovea and Aupark, Bratislava has a few other retail plazas that take care of various preferences and inclinations. Popular choices include Avion Shopping Park, Polus City Center, and Central. These shopping centres offer a blend of worldwide brands, nearby stores, diversion choices, and feasting foundations.

7. Creator Road:
Ventúrska Road and Laurinská Road, by and large known as the Architect Road, are known for their shop stores and displays. Unique

fashion items, jewellery, accessories, and local designer brands can be found here. It's an incredible region to investigate in the event that you're searching for something unmistakable and polished.

These shopping centres provide a wide range of choices to suit a variety of budgets and preferences. Bratislava has something for everyone, whether you're looking for designer clothes, unique souvenirs, or local goods.

Local Products And Souvenirs

Bratislava has a wide selection of local goods and mementos that make excellent gifts or mementos. Consider these well-liked souvenirs and local goods:

1. Slovak Wine: Slovakia has a rich winemaking custom, and you can find various quality wines delivered in the country. Find

bottles of Slovak wine, such as white wines like Riesling or Grüner Veltliner and red wines like Frankovka or Blaufränkisch, on your search.

2. Conventional Specialties: Bratislava is known for its conventional specialties, and you can track down various hand tailored things that grandstand Slovak craftsmanship. Search for unpredictably painted ceramics, wooden toys, weaved materials, and conventional earthenware.

3. Honey-based goods: Slovakia is known for its excellent honey. Search for containers of honey from nearby beekeepers, which frequently come in various flavours and assortments. Honey-based products like beeswax candles and honey-infused cosmetics are also available.

4. Conventional Outfits: Kroje, or folk costumes, are exquisitely crafted and represent the cultural heritage of Slovakia.

Search for small scale variants or extras like weaved belts or headpieces as one of a kind gifts.

5. Čičmany People Craftsmanship: In Slovakia, the village of Imany is well-known for its distinctive folk art, which is characterised by geometric patterns painted on the house facades. Look for items with many-inspired designs, such as ceramics, textiles, or home decor.

6. Blue Church Keepsakes: The Blue Church (St. Elizabeth's Congregation) is a notorious Craftsmanship Nouveau milestone in Bratislava. Find souvenirs like postcards, magnets, or miniature replicas of the church.

7. Slovak Specialties in Food: Bring back some of the traditional dishes that Slovakians eat. Slovak traditional spices and seasonings, such as bryndza (sheep cheese), (plum brandy), and trdelnik (a sweet pastry), should be sought out.

8. Slovak Writing: If you want to learn more about Slovak literature, you might want to pick up a book by a Slovak author or a translation. You can find books in nearby bookshops or keepsake shops.

9. CDs of Folk Music: Search for Compact discs including conventional Slovak people music or contemporary Slovak craftsmen. A wonderful way to bring back a piece of Slovak culture and music are these CDs.

10. Souvenirs with a Bratislava theme: Search for keepsakes that highlight notorious milestones of Bratislava, for example, keychains, mugs, Shirts, or postcards. These items can be found in a lot of souvenir shops all over the city.

While buying gifts, search for marks or signs demonstrating that the items are privately made or true Slovak items. Supporting nearby craftsmans and organisations guarantees that you're getting veritable and excellent gifts while additionally adding to the neighbourhood economy.

Entertainment And Nightlife Bratislava

Bratislava offers a lively diversion and nightlife scene, with various choices to suit various preferences and inclinations. Whether you're searching for unrecorded music, stylish bars, social exhibitions, or late-dance clubs, Bratislava brings something to the table. Here are a few diversion and nightlife choices in Bratislava:

1. Old Town's Pubs and Bars: The vibrant bar scene in the Old Town of Bratislava is well-known. You can find a variety of bars and pubs in the city's squares and narrow streets that serve everything from craft cocktails to local beers. Michalská Street, Venturska

Street, and Sedlárska Street are all popular spots for bar hopping.

2. Unrecorded Music Scenes: There are a number of venues in Bratislava that host live music events, such as jazz clubs, smaller music bars, and concerts. Look at places like Jazz Bistro, Nu Soul Club, or KC Dunaj for a different scope of music kinds and exhibitions.

3. Slovak Public Theater: Bratislava's Slovak National Theatre plays host to opera, ballet, and drama performances. By attending a performance at this renowned venue, you can take in the diverse cultural scene of Slovakia.

4. Film and Film Celebrations: There are a number of movie theatres in Bratislava that show both Slovak and international films. Be on the lookout for film festivals like the Bratislava International Film Festival (BIFF), which present a diverse selection of films from various countries and genres.

5. Danube Stream Travels: Take a relaxing evening cruise on the Danube River to take in the stunning views of the Bratislava skyline lit up at night. A few travels likewise offer unrecorded music, supper, and diversion ready.

6. Nightclubs: There are a lot of clubs in Bratislava that cater to a variety of musical tastes. Appreciate electronic music, hip-bounce, or standard hits at clubs like Radost' Music Club, The Club, or Re: new Club.

7. Casino: Visit one of the city's casinos for some fun gaming if you're lucky. Take a stab at blackjack, roulette, or gambling machines at foundations like Banco Club or Olympic Gambling club Carlton.

8. Festivals and cultural events: Throughout the year, Bratislava hosts a wide range of cultural events and festivals. Check the occasion schedule for shows, craftsmanship

presentations, theatre exhibitions, and other social happenings occurring during your visit.

9. Parody Clubs: At one of the comedy clubs in Bratislava, you can have a good time and laugh all night. Take in a night of laughter and entertainment at stand-up comedy shows that feature comedians from all over the world and from your area.

10. Rooftop eateries and bars: In Bratislava, head to one of the rooftop bars or restaurants for a one-of-a-kind and stylish experience. While sipping cocktails or enjoying a mouthwatering meal, take in the panoramic views of the city.

Visitors to Bratislava will be able to find something enjoyable to do in the evenings because the city's entertainment and nightlife scene caters to a wide range of preferences. Similarly as with any nightlife scene, it's essential to be aware of individual wellbeing and drink capably.

Chapter 3: Cultural and Culinary Experiences

Part 3: Cultural and Culinary Excursions
Bratislava, Slovakia's capital, is home to a diverse cultural and culinary scene that reflects the country's history, customs, and influences. In this part, we will investigate the social and culinary encounters that Bratislava brings to the table, permitting you to drench yourself in the neighbourhood culture and relish the heavenly kinds of Slovak cooking.

1. Exhibition halls and Displays:
Bratislava is home to a scope of historical centres and displays that grandstand its social legacy and creative undertakings. Visit the Slovak Public Historical centre, which houses different displays on Slovak history, antiquarianism, and craftsmanship. The

Slovak Public Exhibition includes an assorted assortment of Slovak and global workmanship, crossing various periods and styles. Try not to miss the Nedbalka Exhibition, known for its advanced and contemporary Slovak craftsmanship.

2. Slovak Public Theater:
Experience the dynamic performing expressions scene at the Slovak Public Theater. Go to an expressive dance, show, or theatre execution to observe the ability of neighbourhood entertainers and drench yourself in the social wealth of Slovakia.

3. Bratislava City Visit:
Take a city tour with a local guide to see the city's most important cultural and historical sites. While learning about the fascinating history and legends of the city, you can visit the Castle, St. Martin's Cathedral, and other notable locations.

4. Traditional and Folkloric Music:

Dig into Slovak old stories and conventional music by going to a live presentation. Experience the lively movies, dazzling music, and vivid ensembles that feature the social customs of Slovakia. Festivals and events that honour Slovak folk culture should be on your radar.

5. Conventional Slovak Cooking:
Try traditional Slovak dishes at local eateries to enjoy the flavours. Goulash, bryndzové halušky (potato dumplings filled with sheep cheese), (sauerkraut soup), or loke (thin potato pancakes) are all delicious options to try. Match your feast with Slovak lagers or test nearby wines from the Little Carpathian wine district.

6. Food and Wine Visits:
To discover Bratislava's culinary delights, take a food or wine tour. Explore traditional eateries, specialty food shops, and local markets. Learn about the production and

significance of regional products like Slovak cheese, cured meats, and pastries.

7. Classes in cooking:
Take a cooking class to immerse yourself in Slovak cuisine. Under the direction of local chefs, learn how to prepare traditional dishes. Enjoy the results of your labour as you learn about the ingredients, methods, and cultural significance of Slovak cooking.

8. Conventional Specialties and Studios:
Visit traditional crafts workshops or studios to learn about the art of Slovak craftsmanship. Learn about the methods used in embroidery, glassmaking, pottery, and woodcarving. You might even get the chance to make your very own piece of Slovak art.

9. Wine sampling in the Little Carpathians:
Visit the Small Carpathian wine region, which is close to Bratislava, for a day trip. Take in wine tastings, visit wineries, and explore vineyards. While taking in the picturesque

countryside, taste the distinctive flavours of Slovak wines, which range from crisp whites to robust reds.

10. Social Celebrations: Bratislava has different social celebrations over time, praising music, expressions, and customs. Events that pay tribute to the city's royal past include the Coronation Festivities, the Bratislava Music Festival, and the Bratislava Christmas Market. These celebrations offer a brief look into the social variety and legacy of Bratislava.

In this chapter, some of Bratislava's cultural and culinary experiences have been highlighted. Embrace the neighbourhood customs, flavours, and creative articulations to drench yourself in the social embroidered artwork of the city completely. Explore Bratislava's diverse cultural and culinary offerings and tailor your experiences to your interests.

Culture And Traditions

Bratislava, the capital city of Slovakia, is rich in culture and traditions that reflect its historical and multicultural heritage. Here are some aspects of Bratislava's culture and traditions that you may find fascinating:

1. Coronation History:
Bratislava has a royal history and was once the coronation city of the Kingdom of Hungary. From the 16th to the 19th centuries, Hungarian kings and queens were crowned in the city's St. Martin's Cathedral. The Coronation Festivities held annually in Bratislava commemorate this royal tradition with reenactments, parades, and historical exhibitions.

2. Folklore and Traditional Music:

Slovak folklore plays a significant role in the country's cultural identity. Bratislava hosts festivals and events that showcase traditional music, dances, and costumes. Folklore groups perform lively dances like the karička and čardáš, accompanied by traditional musical instruments such as the (a long shepherd's flute) and the cimbalom (a hammered dulcimer).

3. Slovak Cuisine:
Slovak cuisine is rooted in hearty, comforting dishes that reflect the country's agricultural heritage. Traditional Slovak foods include bryndzové halušky (potato dumplings with sheep cheese and bacon), (sauerkraut soup with meat), and (filled dumplings). Slovak cuisine often features ingredients like potatoes, cabbage, pork, and dairy products.

4. Bratislava Castle and the Crown Tower:
Bratislava Castle, with its commanding presence overlooking the city, is a symbol of Bratislava's history and culture. The Crown

Tower of the castle holds significance as it was the location where the Hungarian Crown Jewels were stored during the time of the Kingdom of Hungary.

5. Traditional Costumes:
Slovak traditional costumes, known as , vary across different regions of Slovakia. These colourful costumes, adorned with intricate embroidery and accessories, reflect the cultural diversity of the country. The costumes are often worn during folk festivals, weddings, and other traditional celebrations.

6. Slovak Pottery and Crafts:
Slovakia has a rich tradition of pottery and crafts, with various regions known for their distinctive styles. Folk pottery often features intricate patterns and vibrant colours. Skilled craftsmen produce traditional ceramics, carved wooden items, and embroidered textiles that represent the country's artisanal heritage.

7. Christmas Markets:
During the festive season, Bratislava comes alive with Christmas markets. The markets offer a magical atmosphere with wooden stalls selling traditional crafts, delicious treats, and hot mulled wine. Visitors can experience Slovak Christmas traditions, including the lighting of the Christmas tree and the singing of Christmas carols.

8. Slovak Language:
Slovak is the official language of Slovakia, and it is part of the Slavic language family. While English is widely spoken in Bratislava, learning a few basic Slovak phrases can enhance your cultural experience and interactions with locals.

9. Cultural Festivals:
Bratislava hosts numerous cultural festivals throughout the year, celebrating music, arts, literature, and traditions. These festivals showcase local and international artists, performers, and exhibitions, providing a

platform for cultural exchange and appreciation.

10. Wine Culture:

Slovakia has a long history of winemaking, and the Small Carpathian wine region near Bratislava is renowned for its vineyards and wine production. Wine plays a significant role in Slovak culture, and wine festivals and tastings are held to celebrate this tradition.

Embracing the culture and traditions of Bratislava allows you to gain a deeper understanding of the city's heritage and connect with its people. By experiencing the local customs, cuisine, and festivities, you can immerse yourself in the vibrant cultural tapestry of Bratislava.

Festivals And Event

Bratislava has a large number of celebrations and occasions over time, offering guests an opportunity to encounter the city's lively social scene and submerge themselves in different types of craftsmanship, music, customs, and diversion. The following are some notable Bratislava festivals and events:

1. Bratislava Live event: One of Slovakia's most important classical music festivals is the Bratislava Music Festival. It takes place every year in September and October and features world-renowned orchestras, conductors, and soloists performing in prestigious venues like the Reduta Concert Hall and the Slovak National Theatre.

2. Crowning ordinance Merriments: Bratislava's regal history is commended during the Crowning ceremony Merriments, which happen in June. Through parades, historical reenactments, music performances, and exhibitions, the city honours its history as

the site of Hungarian kings' and queens' coronations.

3. Bratislava Christmas Market: During the holiday season, the Old Town of Bratislava is filled with festive cheer thanks to the Bratislava Christmas Market, a cherished event. Traditional crafts, food, mulled wine, and entertainment are available at wooden stalls decorated with lights and decorations from late November to late December. The market likewise includes a wonderful Christmas tree and everyday exhibitions by nearby performers and ensembles.

4. Days in the City: Bratislava City Days occur in the spring, generally in April or May. The occasion praises the establishment of the city and offers different exercises, including direct visits, social exhibitions, shows, and outside shows. It's a fantastic opportunity to learn about the city's history and explore its landmarks.

5. Festival of Jazz for a Day: The One Day Jazz Festival is part of the Bratislava Jazz Days and features a wide range of Slovakian and international jazz musicians. The festival typically occurs in June and features a day of jazz performances at various city venues.

6. Festival Wilsonic: Wilsonic Celebration is an electronic live performance that happens in Bratislava in June. Electronic artists from Slovakia and other European nations are the primary focus of the festival. It provides a stage for experimental and innovative music from techno, house, and electronica, among others.

7. Design Week in Bratislava: Bratislava Design Week is an annual celebration of creative culture and contemporary design. Held in June, it highlights displays, studios, talks, and establishments exhibiting crafted by neighbourhood and worldwide fashioners across different disciplines.

8. Festival of International Films in Bratislava (BIFF): BIFF is an esteemed film celebration that happens in November, highlighting a choice of worldwide movies, narratives, and short movies. The celebration features different realistic works and gives a stage to arising producers.

9. Bratislava City Long distance race: The Bratislava City Marathon, which takes place in April, draws runners from all over the world. The event offers a variety of race distances, including a fun run, a full marathon, and a half marathon, allowing participants to challenge themselves while exploring the city's landmarks.

10. Nuit Blanche at White Night: White Night Nuit Blanche is a contemporary craftsmanship celebration that changes the city with workmanship establishments, light projections, exhibitions, and shows. It happens all of a sudden in October and offers

a special encounter of workmanship in open spaces.

These are only a couple of instances of the celebrations and occasions that Bratislava has consistently. The city's occasion schedule is loaded up with social, creative, and amusement contributions, guaranteeing there is continuously something energising occurring in Bratislava for guests to appreciate.

Food And Drink You May Try in Bratislava

You can savour a wide range of delectable Slovak dishes and beverages when you visit Bratislava. You should try these traditional dishes and drinks:

1. Bryndzové Halušky: Thought about Slovakia's public dish, bryndzové halušky are little potato dumplings presented with an exceptional sheep cheddar called bryndza. Crispy bacon and melted butter are typically topped with them. You must try this hearty and flavorful dish.

2. Kapustnica: Kapustnica is a conventional sauerkraut soup that is regularly delighted during Christmas. Sauerkraut, various types of meat, such as smoked ham or sausage, mushrooms, and spices are used to make it. It's a soothing and exquisite soup with an unmistakable tart flavour.

3. Lokše: Lokše are dainty potato flapjacks frequently filled in as a side dish or a road food nibble. They can be delighted in plain or loaded up with different garnishes, for example, bryndza (sheep cheddar), jam, or poppy seeds. Loke are satisfying and delectably soft.

4. Placky Zemiakové: Zemiakové placky are potato hotcakes produced using ground potatoes blended in with flour, eggs, and preparing. They are fried until they are golden brown and can be served with sour cream or garlic sauce as a side dish or as a main course.

5. Klobása: Klobása alludes to different kinds of Slovak wieners. Typically, they are grilled or fried, seasoned with spices, and made from pork. Served with mustard and fresh bread, klobása is a popular street food.

6. Slivovica: A traditional Slovak plum brandy is called Slivovica. It is a strong alcoholic beverage with a distinct fruity flavour that is made by distilling fermented plums. It is believed to have medicinal properties and is frequently given as a shot.

7. Czech Beverages: You can enjoy a variety of local beers in Slovakia, which has a thriving beer culture. Topvar, Kaltenecker, and Zlat

Baant are a few well-known Slovak beers. Try a variety of styles, including wheat beers, pilsners, and lagers.

8. Demänovka: Demänovka is a natural alcohol created in Slovakia. It is produced using a blend of spices and flavours, bringing about a one of a kind and sweet-smelling drink. Demänovka is frequently consumed as a post-meal digestive.

9. Medovina: Medovina, also known as mead, is a Slovak honey wine. It is made by fermenting honey in water with spices or herbs added occasionally. Medovina is typically consumed on special occasions and has a sweet and distinctive flavour.

10. Trdelník: Trdelnk has become a popular sweet treat in Bratislava despite not being originally from Slovakia. It is made by wrapping rolled dough around a cylinder mould, grilling it, and then coating it with sugar

and sometimes nuts or cinnamon. Trdelník is a brilliant treat to fulfil your sweet tooth.

These are only a couple of instances of the customary food varieties and drinks you can attempt in Bratislava. Investigating the neighbourhood cooking permits you to submerge yourself in Slovak culture and experience the flavours that characterise this district's culinary legacy.

Local Markets And Street Food

There are numerous local markets and street food options in Bratislava where you can try traditional Slovak dishes and find fresh produce. Bratislava's notable markets and street food experiences include the following:

1. The Trhovisko Mileticova Central Market in Bratislava: This huge indoor market is a

clamouring centre of movement where you can track down many new organic products, vegetables, meats, dairy items, and heated merchandise. It's an extraordinary spot to drench yourself in the neighbourhood food scene and connect with merchants.

2. Stará Trnica's Old Market Hall: The Old Market Hall is a historic building in the centre of the Old Town that houses a variety of food stalls, specialty shops, and cafes. Local products, fresh produce, and mouth watering street food like langos (deep-fried dough), (dumplings), and traditional sausages are all available.

3. Markets for farmers: There are a number of farmers' markets in Bratislava that sell fresh goods and produce sourced locally. Popular options include Palackého Street's farmers' market and SNP Square's market, where you can support local farmers and artisans while discovering seasonal ingredients and traditional Slovak goods.

4. Road Food Slows down: There are numerous street food stalls in Bratislava that sell quick and tasty bites as you wander the streets. Keep an eye out for klobása, which are Slovakian sausages served with mustard and bread, lángo, which is deep-fried dough topped with a variety of ingredients, and , which are fried dough balls coated in powdered sugar.

5. Festivals and food trucks: The food truck scene in Bratislava has been growing, and you can now find a variety of food trucks serving a variety of dishes, from traditional Slovak fare to international fare. Watch out for food celebrations, like the FoodPark celebration, where you can test an assortment of road food choices in a single spot.

6. Hviezdoslavovo Square: In the city centre, Hviezdoslavovo Square is a popular gathering place where food stalls and kiosks sell snacks and beverages. During the colder months, eat

a hot dog, crepe, or glass of mulled wine while taking in the lively atmosphere.

7. Bratislava Road Food Park: Situated in the Miserable Janka Kráľa leave, the Road Food Park is an occasional outside scene where food trucks and slows down put in a position to offer a wide cluster of road food choices. You can test everything from burgers and tacos to Asian cooking and sweet treats.

8. Bratislava Christmas Market: During the happy season, the Bratislava Christmas Market turns into a food sweetheart's heaven. Walk around the market and enjoy conventional deals like lokše (potato hotcakes), trdelník (barbecued mixture covered in sugar and cinnamon), broiled chestnuts, and pondered wine.

Investigating nearby business sectors and attempting road food in Bratislava gives a credible and delightful experience. In order to fully immerse yourself in the city's food culture, you'll have the chance to try traditional Slovak dishes, taste the flavours of the area, and interact with friendly vendors.

Best Restaurant In Bratislava

The culinary scene in Bratislava is alive and well, with numerous excellent eateries serving a variety of cuisines. While taste inclinations differ, here are a few profoundly respected cafés in Bratislava that are known for their quality and creative eating encounters:

1. Leader Café: Leader is a Michelin-featured café situated in the core of Bratislava. It is run by well-known Slovak chef Peter Tefánek and offers a refined dining experience that focuses on innovative flavour combinations and contemporary European cuisine.

2. Grand Cru Dining: Another restaurant with a Michelin star impresses with its elegant setting and gourmet menu. It serves modern Slovak cuisine with a creative twist and uses local ingredients and is in the historic Carlton Hotel.

3. Metiansky Pivovar, Bratislava: Bratislavský Meštiansky Pivovar, situated in the Old Town, is a famous decision for those looking for a sample of customary Slovak food. Traditional Slovak dishes like bryndzové haluky (potato dumplings with sheep cheese) and a variety of freshly brewed beers are available at this restaurant and brewery.

4. UFO Eatery: The UFO Restaurant, which is perched atop the SNP Bridge, offers breathtaking views of Bratislava. It's a memorable dining experience because it has a modern interior, a unique location, and a menu that includes Slovak and international dishes.

5. Albrecht Café: The Albrecht Restaurant, which is inside the boutique Albrecht Hotel, has an elegant setting and a menu that showcases sophisticated European cuisine with a touch of Slovak influences. The eatery additionally flaunts a broad wine list.

6. Prašná Bašta: Praná Bata, which is close to the Bratislava Castle, is famous for its historic charm and traditional Slovak food. This medieval-style restaurant's rustic atmosphere is perfect for enjoying game meats, hearty stews, and roasted meats.

7. Citrus Tree: Lemon Tree is a famous veggie lover and vegetarian eatery in Bratislava. It offers a different menu with dishes produced using new, privately obtained fixings. The friendly service and cosy setting of the restaurant add to its appeal.

8. Meštiansky Pivovar: Metiansky Pivovar is a restaurant and brewery that serves delicious Czech and Slovak cuisine alongside the art of

brewing. It includes a scope of specialty lagers and a menu that incorporates conventional dishes as well as worldwide top choices.

It's prudent to reserve a spot ahead of time, particularly for Michelin-featured eateries or well known feasting foundations. These suggestions address simply an example of the different culinary contributions accessible in Bratislava, and there are a lot more cafés to investigate, each with its own novel style and claims to fame.

Useful Phrases And Vocabulary

Here are a few helpful expressions and jargon in Slovak that can prove to be useful during your visit to Bratislava:

1. Good tidings and Fundamental Articulations:

- Hello: Good morning, Ahoj: Dobré ráno, or good morning, Dobré popoludnie
- Goodbye: Dobrý večer
- Farewell: Dovidenia
- If it's not too much trouble: Prosim - I appreciate it: "akujem" means "welcome": Yes, Prosumm: Áno
- No: No, please excuse me: Preparation 2 Food and beverage ordering:
- I'd like to...: Chcel by som...
- What do you suggest?: How about, then?
- Could I at any point see the menu, please?: What's your opinion ?
- I'm vegan or vegetarian: Som vegetarián/vegán
- Glass of water: Beer: Pohár vody Wine by Pivo: Víno
- Espresso: Káva
- Bill, please: likewise, prose 3. Getting Directions:
- Where are you? : Kde je...?

- Excuse me, might you at any point help me?: Do you want to prepare, please?
 - From where are you? Koľko je to ďaleko?
 - Left: On the right, Vavo: Vpravo - Looking ahead: Rovno

4. Shopping:
 - What amount does it cost?: Koľko to stojí?
 - Could I at any point give this a shot?: Môžem si to vyskúšať?
 - Do you have this in an alternate tone/size?: Máte to inú farbu/veľkosť?
 - I'm simply perusing: 5. Len sa obzerám Numbers:
 - 1: Jeden
 - 2: Dva
 - 3: Tri
 - 4: Štyri
 - 5: Päť
 - 10: Desať
 - 20: 100 Dvdasa: Sto
 - 1000: Tisíc

Keep in mind, many individuals in Bratislava communicate in English, particularly in traveller regions, yet knowing a couple of fundamental expressions in Slovak can extend your regard and appreciation for the nearby culture. Due to the fact that Slovak is a Slavic language, its pronunciation may differ from English. Go ahead and for help or explanation if necessary, as local people are by and large well disposed and able to help.

Chapter 4: Practical Information

Section 4: Information for the Real World In this chapter, we will give you some information for the real world to help you get around Bratislava and make the most of your time there. Here are some essential details to keep in mind, including options for transportation, money, and safety tips:

1. Currency: The Euro (€) is Slovakia's official currency. It is prudent to convey some money with you, despite the fact that credit and check cards are generally acknowledged in many foundations. Cash withdrawals can be made easily from any location in the city thanks to ATMs.

2. Language: The authority language of Slovakia is Slovak. While English is spoken by numerous local people, particularly in vacationer regions, learning a couple of essential expressions in Slovak can upgrade your communications and show your appreciation for the nearby culture.

3. Safety: Although Bratislava is generally safe, common safety precautions are always recommended. Watch out for your things, particularly in jam-packed regions or public transportation. Stay away from detached and dim regions around evening time, and utilise authorised taxis or believed transportation administrations.

4. Transportation:
   - Public Transportation: Bratislava has a productive public transportation framework that incorporates transports, cable cars, and trolleybuses. Tickets must be validated upon boarding and can be purchased at ticket machines or kiosks.
   - Taxis: Use reputable ride-hailing services or licensed taxis. In Bratislava, taxis typically have metres, but it's best to ask for an estimate before you get in one.
   - Strolling: The city centre of Bratislava is fairly compact and best explored on foot. Make the most of scenic walks and pedestrian-friendly areas by donning comfortable shoes.

5. Weather: The climate in Bratislava is continental, with warm summers and cold winters. Spring (April to June) and autumn (September to October) are the best times to visit for pleasant weather. Winters can be cold

with occasional snowfall, while summers can be hot.

6. Outlets for electricity: The European two-pin plug (Type C and Type E) is the standard plug type in Slovakia, where the voltage is 230V. You may require a travel adapter if your destination country uses a different voltage or plug type.

7. Zone time: Bratislava works on Focal European Time (CET), which is UTC+1. Slovakia observes Daylight Saving Time from the last Sunday in March until the last Sunday in October, when it switches to Central European Summer Time (CEST), which is UTC+2.

8. Wi-Fi and Web Access: Most lodgings, cafés, and bistros in Bratislava offer free Wi-Fi for clients. Furthermore, you can track down open Wi-Fi areas of interest in specific regions of the city. When connecting to public networks, you should think about using a

virtual private network (VPN) for safe internet access.

9. Numbers for emergencies:
   - General crisis: 112 - The Police 158 - Medical vehicle: 155
   - Fire: 150

10. Traveller Data: Maps, brochures, and details about attractions, events, and guided tours can all be found at the Bratislava Tourist Information Center, which is on Klobucka Street in the Old Town. The staff can help you with any inquiries you might have.

Make sure to really take a look at the most recent tourism warnings and rules before your excursion to guarantee a protected and charming visit. You will be able to make the most of your time in Bratislava and have an unforgettable time exploring the city's rich culture and attractions if you are prepared and knowledgeable.

Safety Tips And Precautions

Wellbeing ought to continuously be fundamentally important while voyaging. Despite the fact that Bratislava is generally safe, it is essential to take certain precautions to ensure a safe and enjoyable visit. Consider the following safety precautions and tips:

1. Remain Alert and Know about Your Environmental elements: Watch out for your assets and be aware of your environmental factors, particularly in jam-packed regions, vacation spots, and public transportation. Displaying expensive items or carrying a lot of cash should be avoided.

2. Utilise Reliable Transportation Services or Licensed Taxis: Use licensed taxis or reputable ride-hailing services if you need to

take a taxi. Make sure the metre is used and the licence number is visible on the taxi. Before you begin your journey, it is advisable to inquire about an estimated fare.

3. Deal with Your Own Possessions: Keep your resources, including travel papers, wallets, and hardware, in a solid spot, for example, a cash belt or an inn safe. Try not to leave your things unattended in open regions.

4. Use populous and well-lit areas: Particularly at night, stick to areas that are well-lit and populated. Stay away from dim roads or secluded regions where the gamble of episodes might be higher.

5. Make your lodging secure: Make sure that the security measures in your lodging are adequate. When you leave, lock your room and use the room safely to store valuables. If accessible, select facilities in all around voyaged regions.

6. Remain Informed: Remain refreshed on neighbourhood news, tourism warnings, and a particular wellbeing data connected with your objective. Learn the phone numbers for emergency services like the police, ambulance, and fire department.

7. Utilise Dependable ATMs: While utilising ATMs, pick those situated in sufficiently bright and populated regions. When entering your PIN, keep your PIN safe and be mindful of your surroundings. It's best to let your bank or credit card company know in advance about your travel plans.

8. Observe Local Laws and Traditions: Learn about the laws, traditions, and cultural considerations of Bratislava. Regard the nearby customs and act suitably out in the open spots.

9. Drink in moderation: If you decide to drink, do so in moderation. Be mindful of your liquor

consumption, particularly in new conditions, to guarantee your own security and prosperity.

10. Rely on Your Senses: Put your faith in your gut instincts. In the event that a circumstance or spot feels dangerous or awkward, eliminating yourself from it is ideal. If you need help, ask people you trust or authorities.

It is essential to keep in mind that although these measures may increase your level of safety, they do not guarantee complete security. It's generally fitting to direct exhaustive examination, heed nearby guidance, and go to proper lengths to guarantee your own wellbeing while at the same time voyaging.

Health Considerations

It's critical to keep your health and well-being in mind when going to Bratislava or any other destination. In order to assist you in maintaining your health during your visit, consider the following factors:

1. Clinical Protection: Make sure you have appropriate travel medical insurance that covers any potential health issues or emergencies before you go to Bratislava. Make sure you are well-versed in the specifics of your coverage and that the appropriate contact information is readily available.

2. Routine Immunizations: Check to see that all of your routine shots are current. Measles, mumps, rubella, diphtheria, tetanus, pertussis, and influenza vaccinations are among these. Verify your vaccination status and discuss any additional vaccinations recommended for your travel with your healthcare provider.

3. Health Insurance for Travel: If you get sick or hurt while you're on your trip, you might

want to look into purchasing travel health insurance that covers expenses for treatment, emergency medical evacuation, and repatriation. It is essential to examine the policy's specifics and comprehend the coverage provided.

4. Medications on prescription: Assuming you take doctor prescribed drugs, guarantee that you have a sufficient stockpile however long your outing might last. Carry a copy of the prescription and them in their original packaging. In the event that you need to seek medical attention, it is also a good idea to keep a list of the generic names of your medications on hand.

5. Diarrhoea in a Traveller: Good hand hygiene, such as washing your hands frequently with soap and water or using hand sanitizers when handwashing facilities are unavailable, can help prevent traveller's diarrhoea. Try not to polish off regular water,

and utilise filtered water for drinking, cleaning teeth, and washing leafy foods.

6. Food Security: Be wary of food cleanliness and security rehearses. Choose newly ready and completely prepared feasts. Try not to eat crude or half-cooked meats, fish, and unpasteurized dairy items. Before eating, peel or wash fruits and vegetables thoroughly in safe water.

7. Protection from Insects: Bratislava may be infested with mosquitoes during certain seasons. Wearing long-sleeved clothing, using insect repellent, and staying in accommodations with windows that have screens or air conditioning are all ways to avoid being bitten by mosquitoes. If needed, think about using bed nets.

8. Sun Insurance: While visiting throughout the late spring months, safeguard yourself from the sun's destructive beams by utilising sunscreen with a high SPF, wearing a cap,

shades, and lightweight, defensive dress. Look for concealment during top daylight hours to forestall burn from the sun and intensity related diseases.

9. Keep hydrated: Drink plenty of fluids, especially if you're exercising or it's hot outside. Convey a reusable water container and top off it with safe drinking water from solid sources.

10. Get Medical Help: On the off chance that you experience any wellbeing worries during your visit in Bratislava, look for clinical exhortation immediately. Visit a nearby facility or emergency clinic, or contact your movement protection supplier for help and direction.

It's prescribed to talk with a medical services proficient or travel medication expert before your outing to get customised wellbeing guidance in light of your clinical history and current wellbeing status. They can give explicit suggestions with respect to immunizations, prescriptions, and wellbeing insurances for your visit to Bratislava.

Local Customs And Etiquette

Your cultural experience in Bratislava will be enhanced and you will be able to interact with the locals in a manner that is polite and respectful if you are aware of and respect the local customs and etiquette. Consider the following guidelines for proper conduct:

1. Greetings: While meeting somebody interestingly, it is standard to shake hands and keep in touch. Use phrases like "dobr de" (good day) and " veer" (good evening) as formal greetings. Unless asked to use their first name, it is polite to address people by their titles, such as "Mr.," "Mrs.," or "Dr."

2. Dining Manner: It is polite to wait for the host or the oldest person to begin eating before you begin when dining in a Slovak home or restaurant. Instead of eating with your hands, use utensils and keep your hands visible on the table. To show your appreciation for the meal, finishing your plate is considered respectful.

3. Code of Dress: Slovaks will quite often dress well for different events, so it's fitting to dress perfectly and keep away from excessively easygoing clothing, particularly in additional proper settings like theatres, upscale eateries, or strict destinations. It is customary to dress modestly and cover your knees and shoulders when going to churches.

4. Politeness: Slovak culture places a high value on politeness. When making a request or receiving assistance, it is customary to say "prism" (meaning "please") and "akujem" (meaning "thank you"). Good manners call for

using these phrases in addition to greetings and goodbye expressions.

5. Private Space: Slovaks for the most part regard individual space. When talking to other people or waiting in line, keep a safe distance. Unless you are invited to do so or have a close relationship with the person, do not touch or hug them.

6. Shoes: It is standard to take off your shoes when it's somebody's home to enter. Traditional establishments and religious sites also follow this custom. To determine whether it is expected, look for clues like a shoe rack or people taking off their shoes.

7. Punctuality: Being reliable is valued in Slovak culture. Respectful behaviour includes showing up on time for appointments, meetings, and social events. It is courteous to let the other person know in advance if you anticipate being late.

8. Social Behavior: Keep a deferential and obliging disposition openly. Avoid being disruptive or loud, especially in places like museums, libraries, and religious institutions. The majority of indoor public areas prohibit smoking, so designated smoking areas should be utilised whenever possible.

9. Photography: While taking photos, be aware of neighbourhood customs and protection. Before taking pictures of people, especially in more private or religious settings, it is polite to ask permission.

10. Tipping: Tipping is standard in Bratislava. If you received excellent service, it is customary to leave a 10% tip at restaurants, cafes, and bars. Taxi drivers, tour guides, and hotel staff are all welcome to be rewarded, but it is not required.

By monitoring and deferential towards nearby traditions and behaviour, you can cultivate positive connections with local people and exhibit your appreciation for Slovak culture during your visit to Bratislava.

Currency And Money Matters

Cash and cash matters are fundamental contemplations while visiting Bratislava. Here is a data to assist you with exploring cash trade and cash related viewpoints during your excursion:

1. Currency: The Euro (€) is Slovakia's official currency. It is broadly acknowledged all through Bratislava, and most foundations, including lodgings, cafés, shops, and vacation destinations, will acknowledge instalment in Euros.

2. Change of Currency: You can trade your money to Euros at banks, trade workplaces (known as "zmenáreň"), or approved cash trade corners. Banks commonly offer serious trade rates, however they might have restricted working hours. Trade workplaces are many times tracked down in vacationer regions and deal more adaptable hours yet may charge higher expenses or proposition less ideal rates. Before making a currency exchange, it's a good idea to compare rates and fees.

3. ATMs: The majority of Bratislava's ATMs, or automatic teller machines, accept major credit and debit cards from around the world. They make it simple to withdraw cash in Euros. Notwithstanding, be aware of any related expenses charged by your bank or card supplier for worldwide withdrawals. Educate your bank regarding your itinerary items ahead of time to stay away from any issues with your card.

4. Credit and Charge Cards: In Bratislava, especially in larger establishments like hotels, restaurants, and retail stores, credit and debit cards are widely accepted. The most widely accepted card networks are Visa and Mastercard, while American Express and Discover may have less widespread acceptance. For smaller establishments or places that may not accept credit cards, it is recommended to bring some cash with you.

5. Tipping: Tipping is standard in Bratislava, however it isn't required. In cafés, it's not unexpected to leave a tip of around 10% of the all out bill on the off chance that you got great help. You can pass on the tip in real money or add it to the last sum while paying via card. Before leaving a second tip, check to see if there is a service charge included in the bill. Taxi drivers, hotel staff, and tour guides all receive tips for excellent service.

6. Wellbeing and Security: Take precautions to safeguard your money and other valuables.

Passports, additional cash, and important documents can all be stored in hotel safes. Be wary of pickpockets and keep an eye on your belongings in crowded areas. Try not to show enormous amounts of cash in broad daylight and utilise secure ATMs situated in sufficiently bright and populated regions.

7. Trade Rates: Remain refreshed on the ongoing trade rates to guarantee you are getting fair worthwhile trading money or making instalments. For quick reference, you can check exchange rates online or use currency converter apps.

8. Little Change: Keep some more modest category notes and coins with you for more modest buys, public transportation, or tipping purposes. It's valuable to have various groups to keep away from hardships while rolling out definite improvements.

Make sure to illuminate your bank or Visa supplier of your itinerary items to forestall any disturbances to your card use. In the event of unforeseen circumstances, it is also a good idea to carry a backup method of payment, such as an additional credit card or some extra cash.

By being aware of cash and cash matters, you can explore monetary exchanges flawlessly during your visit to Bratislava and have an issue free encounter dealing with your costs.

How To Save Money In Bratislava Vacation

Setting aside cash during your excursion in Bratislava can assist you with taking advantage of your spending plan and stretch your assets further. Here are a few hints to assist you with setting aside cash while as yet partaking in your time in the city:

1. Accommodation:
   - Look for accommodations that are affordable: Consider staying in guesthouses, lodgings, or spending plan lodgings that deal lower rates contrasted with lavish inns.
   - Book ahead of time: You might be able to take advantage of early bird discounts or other special offers if you book your lodging in advance.

2. Transportation:
   - Use public transportation: Buses, trams, and trolleybuses are all part of the dependable and reasonably priced public transportation system in Bratislava. Buy day or multi-day travel cards for limitless rides, which can be more financially savvy than individual tickets.
   - Cycle or walk: Bratislava's downtown area is conservative and effectively walkable. Save money on transportation by exploring the city's attractions by walking or cycling.

3. Eating and Food:
   - Eat like a neighbourhood: When compared to posh dining establishments, local eateries, cafes, and street food stalls offer traditional Slovak fare at prices that are more reasonable.
   - Look into local markets: You can find fresh produce, snacks, and local specialties at lower prices at local markets like the Bratislava Central Market and the Old Market Hall than in tourist areas.
   - Living on your own: If your room has a kitchenette, you might want to think about making some of your meals with items from local markets or grocery stores. Dining costs could be cut down as a result.

4. Attractions and sights to see:
   - Exploit free attractions: Bratislava offers a few free attractions, like St. Martin's House of Prayer, the Blue Church, and Bratislava Palace gardens. Investigate these locales to partake in the city's set of experiences and

culture without burning through cash on extra charges.

- Make use of discount passes or city cards: Consider buying city cards or markdown passes that give admittance to different attractions at a limited cost. Commonly, these cards also include free use of public transportation.

5. Diversion and Exercises:

- Look for events that are free or cheap: For free concerts, festivals, or exhibitions during your visit, check the listings for local events. There are a lot of cultural events that are free or have low entry fees.

- Appreciate outside exercises: Bratislava offers lovely parks and outside spaces where you can appreciate picnics, strolls, or bicycle rides without burning through cash on costly amusement choices.

6. Shopping and Trinkets:

- Visit local markets to shop: Instead of shopping at tourist-oriented stores, look for souvenirs, traditional crafts, or local goods at prices that are more affordable at local markets or smaller shops.

- Compare prices and bargain: While shopping in business sectors or more modest shops, go ahead and arrange costs or contrast costs across various merchants with guarantee you are getting the best incentive for your cash.

Be sure to prepare a budget in advance and keep track of your trip expenses. You can make your Bratislava vacation more affordable while still enjoying the city's attractions, culture, and cuisine by implementing these money-saving strategies.

Things To Pack And Dress Code In Bratislava

Take into consideration the expected weather, planned activities, and cultural norms when packing for your trip to Bratislava. Here is a rundown of things to pack and clothing standard rules for Bratislava:

1. Clothing:
   - Happy with strolling shoes: The city centre of Bratislava is best explored on foot, so bring comfortable shoes to walk the cobblestone streets and see the city's sights.
   - Clothing with layers: Pack clothes that can be worn in layers to deal with changing weather. Bratislava encounters blistering summers and cold winters, so be ready for both warm and cool temperatures.
   - Downpour coat or umbrella: It's a good idea to bring a lightweight rain jacket or a small umbrella with you in case it rains occasionally in Bratislava.
   - Dressier clothing: On the off chance that you intend to visit upscale cafés, theatres, or go to comprehensive developments, pressing

some dressier clothing, for example, a decent dress or savvy relaxed outfits is suggested.

2. Climate Contemplations:
   - Summer: For the hot summer months (June to August), bring clothing that is light and breathable, like t-shirts, shorts, dresses, or skirts. For sun protection, don't forget to bring a hat, sunglasses, and sunscreen.
   - During the winter months (December through February), Bratislava can experience temperatures below freezing. To keep yourself warm in the cold, bring layers, a coat, hat, gloves, scarves, and warm clothing.
   - Spring and Fall: These seasons (Walk to May and September to November) can have gentle temperatures. To accommodate varying weather conditions, pack a mix of lightweight and warmer clothing, such as long-sleeved shirts, lightweight sweaters, and jackets.

3. Social Contemplations:

- Dress with respect: It's best to dress modestly when going to churches, religious sites, or more formal places. This might incorporate covering your shoulders and knees, and abstaining from uncovering or provocative dress.

- Swimsuits: Assuming you intend to visit pools or warm showers, pack suitable swimwear.

- Embellishments: Remember to pack basics like a cap, shades, and an agreeable daypack or sack for conveying your things during touring.

4. Down to earth Things:

- Adapter for travel: If your devices use a different type of plug or voltage, you should bring a travel adapter with you to Bratislava because it uses the European two-pin plug.

- Prescriptions and medications: Pack any essential drugs in their unique bundling, alongside duplicates of solutions and significant clinical reports.

- Travel fundamentals: For backup, bring a photocopy of important documents, information about travel insurance, local currency or credit/debit cards, and a valid passport.

Make sure to really take a look at the weather conditions gauge before your outing and change your pressing likewise. Likewise, consider the exercises you intend to take part in, like climbing or open air undertakings, and pack fitting stuff and footwear.

You'll be ready to enjoy your time in Bratislava while remaining comfortable and respectful of local customs by packing a variety of comfortable clothes, keeping cultural norms in mind, and being prepared for the weather.

Do's And Don'ts In Bratislava

While visiting Bratislava, it's useful to know about the nearby traditions and decorum to guarantee a positive and conscious experience. Here are some would's and don'ts to keep in care:

Do's:
1. Always shake hands with people and keep your eyes on them.
2. Do address individuals utilising their titles (Mr., Mrs., Dr.) trailed by their last name, except if welcome to utilise their most memorable name.
3. Do say "prosím" (please) and "ďakujem" (thank you) while making demands or getting help.
4. Do attempt to get familiar with a couple of essential expressions in Slovak, like good tidings and much obliged.
5. Do dress humbly and consciously, particularly while visiting holy places or strict locales.

6. Take the necessary precautions against pickpockets and be mindful of your possessions.
7. During your time in the country, don't forget to try some local dishes and traditional Slovak fare.
8. Do regard the climate by discarding waste appropriately and observing any posted guidelines in parks and public spaces.
9. When you are in public places like lines or on public transportation, be courteous and patient.

Don'ts:
1. Unless asked, do not address people by their first name.
2. Try not to bite gum or smoke where it is restricted.
3. Unless you have established a close relationship with the person with whom you are speaking, you should not discuss political issues or contentious historical events, which are sensitive topics.

4. Avoid taking pictures of people without their permission, especially in religious or intimate settings.
5. Avoid being overly boisterous or disruptive in public settings, particularly those where silence or respect are expected.
6. In churches or other religious locations, unless directed to do so, do not move or touch religious objects or artefacts.
7. Avoid littering and leaving behind trash. For disposal, use designated bins.
8. Try not to expect everybody to communicate in English fluidly. Even though many people speak English, learning a few basic Slovak phrases is always appreciated.

By following these do's and don'ts, you can recognize the nearby culture, collaborate emphatically with local people, and take full advantage of your time in Bratislava. Keep in mind that being mindful and considerate makes a big difference in making a good impression and encouraging cultural exchange.

Common Scam In Bratislava

Despite the fact that Bratislava is generally a safe city, it's important to be aware of common tourist scams. By being educated, you can all the more likely safeguard yourself and try not to succumb to tricks. The following are a couple of normal tricks to be mindful of in Bratislava:

1. Scam Taxis: Some taxi drivers may overcharge tourists who aren't expecting it, especially tourists who aren't familiar with the rates in their area. To stay away from this, utilisation authorised taxis or trustworthy ride-flagging down administrations, or ask your lodging or eatery to orchestrate a dependable taxi for you. Guarantee that the

metre is utilised and request an expected admission prior to beginning your excursion.

2. Counterfeit Cops: Be careful in the event that somebody professing to be a cop approaches you and requests to see your identification or individual possessions. Always make sure to ask for proof of identity, and if you have any doubts, you can tell them to go to the nearest police station to get the problem fixed. Genuine law enforcement personnel will not object to your cautious approach.

3. Cash Trade Tricks: Pay attention to unofficial exchange offices when exchanging currency because they may charge high fees or offer unfavourable rates. Before making any transactions, make sure you use reputable exchange offices or banks and compare rates and fees. Pay careful attention to the current exchange rates and count your money.

4. Theft by distraction: People who might try to distract you by asking for directions or pretending to spill something should be avoided. While you are occupied, an associate could attempt to take your possessions. Watch out for your possessions, particularly in packed regions, and use sacks with secure terminations.

5. Skimming ATMs: Be on the lookout for any suspicious devices that are attached to the card reader or keypad when using ATMs. Skimming devices may be used by criminals to steal your card information. In the event that you notice anything uncommon, track down another ATM or advise the bank right away.

6. Pickpocketing: Like in any bustling traveller objective, pickpocketing can happen in packed regions, public transportation, or famous vacationer destinations. Be aware of your surroundings and secure your valuables.

Keep important documents like passports safe and use bags with anti-theft features.

To safeguard yourself from tricks, it's prudent to utilise sound judgement, pay attention to your gut feelings, and be mindful while managing new circumstances or people. Remain informed about normal tricks, heed neighbourhood guidance, and report any dubious exercises to the proper specialists. By being proactive and mindful, you can limit the dangers and partake in a protected and pleasant visit to Bratislava.

Conclusion

All in all, Bratislava offers a rich mix of history, culture, and regular magnificence, making it an enamoring objective for explorers. From its intriguing history and compositional miracles to its dynamic social scene and scrumptious cooking, Bratislava brings a lot to the table for guests.

In this aide, we take care of different parts of arranging your excursion to Bratislava, including its set of experiences, geology, environment, top attractions, open air exercises, shopping, diversion, social encounters, and culinary enjoyments. We have likewise given reasonable data on transportation, convenience, visa prerequisites, and security tips to guarantee a smooth and pleasant visit.

To fully immerse yourself in the city's distinctive atmosphere, remember to respect local customs and etiquette as you explore Bratislava, sample the local cuisine, and participate in cultural activities. Whether you're walking around the beguiling Old Town, partaking in the beautiful excellence of the Danube Waterway, or enjoying conventional Slovak dishes, Bratislava offers a great blend of encounters for each voyager.

You will be able to make the most of your time in Bratislava and create memories that will last a lifetime if you are prepared, respectful, and willing to try new things. Make the most of your trip to this charming city!

Printed in Great Britain
by Amazon